St Andrews: Portrait of a City

Peter Adamson & Lorn Macintyre

Text ©2007   Lorn Macintyre.   Photography ©2007   Peter Adamson.

First published in the United Kingdom in 2004 by Alvie Publications, 52 Buchanan Gardens, Si Andrews, Fife KT169LX Tel: 01334 475227

3rd and revised edition 2008

Printed and bound in China by Imago.

ISBN 0-9511800-3-7

Aspiring alpinists can practise their climbing skills on the Rock and Spindle, on the St Andrews to Kingsbarns coastal walk. The formation takes its name from its similarity to a huge spinning wheel, the tall pillar representing the distaff or rock,the wheel-shaped projection being the spindle.

Acknowledgements

For providing the Foreword, special thanks to Brian Lang, Principal, St Andrews University. For help with providing information and checking text, thanks to the following members of the University: Norman Reid, Keeper of Muniments; Rachel Hart, University Library Special Collections; Helen Rawson, Curator, Museum Collections; Louise Taylor, Assistant Director of Development; Lorraine Fraser, Academic Registrar; John Frew, Art History; Lesley Lind, Publications; Gayle Cook, Press Office.

Valuable services have been rendered by: Dawn White, photographer; Edwina Proudfoot, archaeologist; Edith Cormack and Bob Mitchell, St Andrews Botanic Garden; Elizabeth Williams, St Andrews Preservation Trust; Tom Gardner, the Byre Theatre; Lizzie Hazlehurst, British Golf Museum; Angela Howe, Royal & Ancient Golf Club; Alexander Walsh, Kate Kennedy Club; Professor John Guy, Clare College, Cambridge.

Thanks to: James Allan, pilot; University janitors; Bute Photographic Unit; Byre Theatre; L.S.G. Matheson, Rector of Madras College; Robert Tims, Headmaster, St Leonards School; Andrew Donald, Headmaster, New Park School; Katie and Malcolm Bennie; Clare Benskin; David Brown; Sophie Butler; Hayley-Joy Cawthorne; Sandy Edwards; Shopna Farhad; Lewis Hazel; Sarah Grieve; Ellie Griffith; Fraser MacDonald; Gordon McMullan; Jon Marsh; Nigel Mattison; Angus McLean; Susan Millar; Chetan Morjaria; Claire O'Donnell; Martin Passmore; Ibukun and Neil Strachan; John Standberg; Clare Turner; Juliette Carswell; Andrew Pearson; Bonnie Cryer; Sandra Wallace; Laura Thatcher; Martin Dyer; Susannah Glynn; Charis Robertson; Robert Bartlett; Will McGowan; Sally Crumplin; Paul Field; Mary Macintyre.

Thanks to Evelyn Simpson, for her permission to use her photograph on the cover. For permission to quote from George Bruce's poem A Gateway to the Sea (1), thanks to David Bruce and to Marjorie Bruce (Inglis). Karen Gourlay of Purplepoint took great care in preparing this book for publication.

Introduction

St Andrews is Scotland's Camelot. As you drive towards it from the north-west on a summer's afternoon the spires and towers on the horizon shimmer in the haze from the North Sea, as if this is an enchanted place that doesn't belong in the 21st century. But as you approach you see dozens of golfers trundling their trolleys of fibre-shafted clubs across the immaculate links, and you pass hotels and student residences of striking modernity. St Andrews has adapted and expanded down the centuries without losing its unique character, its aura of history, which is why all roads that lead to it are busy all summer long.

Who were the early settlers in this part of Scotland? Hunter gatherer sites at Morton Lochs and at Fife Ness have provided evidence of people who built light huts for temporary camps, who had log boats to catch deep-water fish, collected shellfish and berries and hunted deer -a diet nutritionists would approve for us today.

Farmers reached Fife before 3000BC, and there are remains of their settlements and fields. Their flint arrowheads, flint and stone axes have been found in St Andrews and the surrounding area, while the Bronze Age is represented by many rich burial sites, such as the one at Lawhead, where there was a beautiful necklace of polished shale beads, as well as a great many burial urns.

Although many Roman artefacts have been found in the area the only Roman sites in Fife are temporary camps; that at Edenwood, west of Cupar, seems to have been built on a native site, and several houses and hilltop sites can be seen in the vicinity. Two burials with Roman jewellery were found at the Pictish long cist cemetery at the Hallow Hill, a mile inland. These date mainly to the seventh century, and suggest early Christian missionary activity.

St Rule is said to have landed at Kilrymont, bringing relics of St Andrew with him, and the Pictish king donated 'the head of the king's ridge', part of his hunting grounds, to establish a church, which grew to become the Priory, the remains of which are still impressive.

Over the centuries St Andrews developed into a town. Now it is a city, spreading into the surrounding farmland, with a university of over seven thousand students and academic staff, and hundreds of thousands of visitors each year. It is one of the most desirable places in Scotland to live in because, despite the pressures from traffic, the centre of the city is still unspoilt, retaining many of its old buildings. This book will allow you to wander through it.

The families have left the West Sands, and the sun is setting. Soon the tide will erase the furrows and footprints.

Foreword

A first time visitor to St Andrews, accustomed to the urban sprawl that is common in Britain, will be immediately struck by the quality of light in this corner of North East Fife. The distant absence of smoke-stack industry, and the ever present North Sea breeze, combine with a townscape that has its origins many centuries ago, to produce a visual adventure.

Peter Adamson has caught St Andrews in a feast of images, representing not just its physical characteristics but its cosmopolitan population of students and academics, golfers, shop keepers and all manner of townspeople and visitors. Peter has been photographing St Andrews for many years, and knows the town and its inhabitants as well as anyone. The Scottish writer Lorn Macintyre, who is a St Andrews resident and local historian, has provided the captivating text and captions.

St Andrews is one of the birthplaces of photography, so this is a highly appropriate book. It will deserve frequent revisiting by all of us, and it is comforting to know that we will be enjoying Peter Adamson images of St Andrews for many years to come.

Brian Lang MA, PhD
Principal and Vice-Chancellor
University of St Andrews

Dr Brian Lang, Principal and Vice-Chancellor of the University of St Andrews, chats to a graduate who needs no introduction.

The Early Church

St Andrews is really one man's dream, or so legend insists. It seems that an angel appeared to a Greek monk called Rule or Regulus. Andrew, the fisherman from Galilee and one of Christ's disciples, had been killed by the Romans in Patras, Southern Greece, for spreading the gospel, martyred on the cross that was to be adopted as the Scottish Saltire.

The angel instructed Rule to take some of the mortal remains of Andrew to 'the ends of the earth' for safe-keeping,because they were going to be transferred to Constantinople. The mysterious Greek monk must have had anatomy skills, or access to a competent anatomist, to be able to remove a tooth, an arm bone, a kneecap and some finger bones from St Andrew's body.

It has been claimed that Rule's voyage westward with this macabre cargo took eighteen months, and that it ended when he and his companions waded ashore in the St Andrews area, already one of the oldest Christian sites in Scotland, and with a Pictish royal residence.

St Andrew's relics were then placed in the Pictish monastery at Kilrymont (the church of the King's Muir), which is believed to have been founded by the Pictish warrior-king Unust in the mid 8th century.

An alternative legend, less attractive, is that Acca, Bishop of Hexham, a renowned collector of relics, brought the relics of St. Andrew to Fife in 733.

After the founding of St Andrews Cathedral in the 12th century the Saint's relics were transferred to the massive splendour of the new place of worship. The presence of the shrine of Scotland's premier Saint, a favourite of royal patrons, made St Andrews one of the great centres of religion in medieval Europe. The journey to the shrine must have been a hazardous one, on foot or horseback, through forests inhabited by wild animals and bandits. But faith prevailed over fear.

St Andrews Cathedral was wrecked in the Reformation, and the relics of St Andrew disappeared. Is it possible that some of them – a tooth, a finger bone - are still among the surviving ruins, awaiting archaeologists of the future? Or will they be scattered dust by now?

St Andrews Cathedral

The fifth of July 1318 was a busy day in St Andrews. Nobles in their finery congregated from all over Scotland to witness their King, otherwise known as Robert the Bruce, consecrate the new Cathedral. Those who had not seen it before must have gasped at the scale. Paced out inside, it was 357 feet long. The cathedral had a 12 bay nave, and a choice of chapels where the visitors could kneel at their devotions in the royal ceremony. Beyond the high altar the relics of St Andrew were housed.

The construction had suffered setbacks since Arnold, Abbot of Kelso, founded the Cathedral in 1160. The newly built west gable had been brought down by a gale, and in 1304 Edward 1 had ordered the lead roof to be stripped off and melted down into munitions for the siege of Stirling.

But on that July day of dedication in 1318 the singing of the congregation must have raised the roof. The chalice that touched the lips of the King of Scots would have been pure gold.

Pilgrims from all over Scotland and beyond, seeking a cure from an illness or a remission from a sin, arrived to kneel at the cathedral's many altars, and at the shrine of St Andrew. Then the horses of the Reformers hurried towards St Andrews. Sunday 11th June 1559 was the day of reckoning. For three days John Knox ranted against Catholicism to the assembled Protestant Lords. The wreckers headed for the Cathedral with their hammers, determined to smash idolatry. A bonfire was made of wooden statues, and the tombs plundered.

A cloaked figure used to wander the cathedral site towards the close of the 19th century. But it wasn't the ghost of a monk mourning the destruction of one of the wonders of the age. John, 3rd Marquis of Bute, Rector of the University of St Andrews, was fascinated by ecclesiastical sites, and considered diverting part of his fabulous fortune from coal to rebuilding the Cathedral. It was probably fortunate that his dream was abandoned, because we can reconstruct the thirty acre site in our imagination.

The wrecked Cathedral provided St Andrews with a quarry from which to build some of its dwellings.

(Opposite page): This magnificent head was found in the monastic latrine in 1894, along with two others, presumably thrown there at the Reformation in contempt at 'idolatrous' images. Clearly the head of Christ, what happened to the major statue of which it must have been a part?

Thursday 19th August 1773. 'It was a very fine day. Dr. Johnson seemed quite wrapt up in the contemplation of the scenes which were now presented to him. He kept his hat off while he was upon any part of the ground where the cathedral had stood. He said well, that "Knox had set on a mob, without knowing where it would end; and that differing from a man in doctrine was no reason why you should pull his house about his ears."' (James Boswell, The Journal of a Tour to the Hebrides with Samuel Johnson, LL.D.).

The Church of St Rule once gave sanctuary to the pilgrim arriving in St Andrews. Now visitors can climb to the top to view the extent of the Cathedral.

In the Cathedral cemetery local citizens lie beside the great and good.

St Leonard's Chapel

One of St Andrews's best kept secrets, the charming chapel of St Leonard's is tucked inside the grounds of the school which bears the Saint's name.

Originally the parish church of St Leonard in the early 15th century, the building was reconstructed, using 12th century masonry, in the early 16th century, when it became part of St Leonard's College, with a choir for college use, and nave for parochial services.

In 1747 the buildings of St Leonard's College were abandoned after its amalgamation with St Salvator's College. In 1761 the parish congregation of St Leonard's Chapel followed the students to the larger St Salvator's Chapel. St Leonard's Chapel lost its roof and its west tower. However, its bell was salvaged and transferred to St Salvator's Tower, from where it can still be heard.

In 1773, during his journey to the Western Isles, Samuel Johnson observed of the St Leonard's Chapel remains: 'A decent attempt has been made... to convert it into a kind of green-house... the plants do not hitherto prosper. To what use it will next be put I have no pleasure in conjecturing.'

In the early decades of the 19th century St Leonard's Chapel suffered further humiliation with the demolition of its west bay in order to improve access from South Street. But the building was re-roofed and reglazed in 1910. Its total restoration in the middle of the 20th century was due to the generosity of the Pilgrim Trust, and to the munificence of the Russell family, Markinch papermakers who have been major benefactors to the University. Sir David Russell helped to restore St Leonard's Chapel in memory of his son John Patrick (Pat), a former St Andrews student, killed in action in Italy in 1944.

The Chapel is an exquisite small building of great historical interest, with monuments, including one of an anonymous 'chief master of the poor students,' with incised full-length effigy. The building is open on specific days throughout the year, and during the University terms Compline by Candlelight on Thursdays at 10pm is a wonderfully intimate spiritual experience.

St Leonard's Chapel is a popular venue for weddings and other celebrations. The presiding Minister is the Reverend Dr Jamie Walker, Chaplain of the University of St Andrews since 1993, an inspirational preacher tireless in his efforts to alleviate the personal problems of students, and to ensure that they are happy and fulfilled during their time at St Andrews.

One of the most familiar landmarks in St Andrews, the surviving north transept of the 16th century Dominican convent church of Blackfriars on South Street has always attracted the camera. This is said to have been the first building to have been vandalised during the Reformation, and its fragmented presence reminds us of what has been lost.

The view of the Blackfriars relic from Madras College grounds.

The tower of the late medieval Church of the Holy Trinity, founded by Bishop Wardlaw in 1410-12, survived the building's 'drastic' reconstruction of 1798 - 1800. On a summer afternoon of milling tourists and traffic, step inside, to be uplifted by the arched interior, the wealth of 19th century stained glass.

A sombre memorial in an eerie setting at Magus Muir, where James Sharp, Archbishop of St Andrews, was murdered on 3rd May 1679. The University Rector, 'ushered by three macers,' gave the Archbishop a fitting send-off at his funeral.

St Andrews Castle

The ruins of St Andrews Castle look as old as the nearby Cathedral, but date mainly from the 16th century. There was, however, an older castle on the site, erected circa 1200 by Bishop Roger as his residence, as befitting the Cathedral's chief dignitary. Perhaps there was a far earlier habitation there, occupied by the shellfish eaters before the arrival of the Saint's relics turned St Andrews into a place of significance.

During the Wars of Independence the castle was captured and recaptured, dismantled and rebuilt, with both the Scots and the English having a hand in these transformations. After Bannockburn (1314) the castle was in Scottish hands again.

But the English were persistent. They took the castle again, and rebuilt it in 1336. In 1337 Sir Andrew Moray, Warden of Scotland, hauled his engines of war to St Andrews and 'mightily besieged the castle thereof for three weeks…and to erd syn dang in doun.' In other words, its stones were once again scattered.

Bishop Wardlaw, founder of the university, tutored James 1 in the rebuilt castle, and came to live there in 1425. However, James Beaton, Archbishop of St Andrews, seems to have been the biggest spending tenant of the castle, when he lived in it from 1523 to 1539. The English ambassador wrote in wonder – or envy – that the Bishop 'gave livery nightly to twenty-one score horses.'

The Bishop's nephew didn't sleep so soundly in the castle. Cardinal David Beaton needled Henry V111, and the castle was besieged. The body of the murdered cardinal was hung from a wallhead.

For those with claustrophobia, the castle's Bottle Dungeon must have been hell, with 'many of God's children… imprisoned' in its depth, according to John Knox.

When the 2nd Earl of Arran laid siege to the castle he was backed by a French fleet and by cannon mounted on the Cathedral tower, and on the tower of St Salvator's Church. To augment this aerial assault, the determined Earl had a passageway blasted through the rock in order to gain entry to the castle. Admission, via Historic Scotland's stylish visitor centre, is easier today.

According to local historian Dr Hay Fleming, this well at St Andrews Castle was rediscovered in 1857. A plumb-line established its total depth at 51 feet 7 inches (not all water). By 1887 the depth had shortened to 35 feet 3 inches because children had been dropping stones down the well to make a big splash. In 1903, when the well was cleaned out, two imperfect gargoyles were found in it.

Not a place to spend the night: the countermine at St Andrews Castle, constructed to thwart the excavations of the 2nd Earl of Arran, who had a mine dug to breach the castle's defences when he laid siege to it in 1546-47. Both mine and countermine were rediscovered in 1879 during foundation work on a house in the vicinity of the castle.

University of St Andrews

On 3rd February 1414 a series of Papal Bulls arrived in St Andrews. Did they come by horseback, or were they handed ashore from a boat? However it was, the following day, a Sunday, the Bulls were promulgated in the presence of a great assembly in the Refectory of the Priory, followed by Te Deum in the Cathedral, to give thanks for the foundation of Scotland's first university.

Today's typical student is a late teenager. Those who arrived in St Andrews with their trunks in the Middle Ages would probably have been about thirteen. They were expected to have a thorough grounding in grammar before beginning their studies of logic and rhetoric.

By the middle of the sixteenth century the University of St Andrews had three colleges - St Salvator's (1450), St Leonard's (1512), and St Mary's (1538). It was an all-male institution. St Leonard's College was monastic in character, with the students strictly supervised and segregated from the outside world. No woman was to be allowed inside the College except the laundress, and she had to be at least 50 years old.

When Protestantism triumphed in Scotland in August 1560 the Reformers set out their scheme for university reform in the First Book of Discipline, and made it clear that they wanted to reconstruct, rather than abolish, the University of St Andrews. In fact, it was to be the 'first and principal' of the three universities (St Andrews, Glasgow and Aberdeen) detailed in the scheme.

But the Reformers' plans for St Andrews were not implemented, and teaching was disrupted as the zealots removed the 'Popish' influence from the university. James Melville kept a diary in which he recorded his hero-worship of John Knox, but also his activities in 'archerie and goff.' James's uncle Andrew Melville was Principal of St Mary's College from 1580 to 1607, and Professor of Divinity ex officio by virtue of his appointment as Principal. He became Rector of the University in 1590, and is remembered for his statesmanship which helped to preserve the judicial privileges of the University.

Melville transformed St Mary's College into one of the foremost schools of Protestant theology in Europe, and instigated new standards of scholarship in the University. However, four years after the accession of James to the joint thrones of England and Scotland in 1603, Melville was sent to the Tower of London. He remained in prison for four years, and was released to go to Sedan to occupy the collegiate Chair of Divinity at Sedan University, instead of returning to the University of St Andrews.

The Collegiate Church of St Salvator survived the Reformation. Dr Ronald Cant wrote in The University of St Andrews, a Short History that 'Even after all the changes of five hundred years, the Church remains one of the most remarkable examples of Gothic art in Scotland. The great vaulted roof has long since disappeared, likewise the original window tracery, and all the wealth of costly furnishings with which it was equipped by its Founder [Bishop James Kennedy]; but the tomb which Kennedy prepared for himself is still there, sadly battered, but the finest thing of its kind in Scotland, a fitting monument to the most splendid and cultured Scotsman of his age.'

Inspired by French design, and probably executed by French craftsmen using stone shipped across the Tay estuary from Angus, Kennedy's tomb-chest has a black marble top, and a bronze front of 20th century origin.

Andrew Lang, the bard of St Andrews ('a haunted town it is for me') and a graduate of the University also has his monument here, in the form of a bronze portrait relief on the North Wall.

The Act of Union of 1707 and the abolition of episcopacy in the established church damaged the status of the University of St Andrews. However, the curriculum and the matriculation roll of St Andrews expanded over the years, with the development of teaching and research in the Arts, Divinity, and the Biological and Physical Sciences.

University College, Dundee, was established in 1881 and affiliated to, and partially incorporated within the University of St Andrews from 1897, a fertile association terminated in 1967 with the foundation of a separate University of Dundee.

The University of St Andrews, with over seven thousand students and academic staff, its old buildings preserved, and new ones built around the city, has an international reputation for academic excellence, and is probably the most attractive campus in Scotland.

Is Sir Menzies Campbell, Leader of the Liberal Democrat Party, and Chancellor of the University of St Andrews, rehearsing a Conference speech under the expert tutelage of honorary graduate Joanna Lumley?

Thanks to the generosity of local philanthropist Mrs Cookie Matheson, who paid for new clocks for St Salvator's tower, students now have no excuse for being late for lectures.

Bishop Henry Wardlaw, founder of the University, looks down on students dining in St Salvator's Hall.

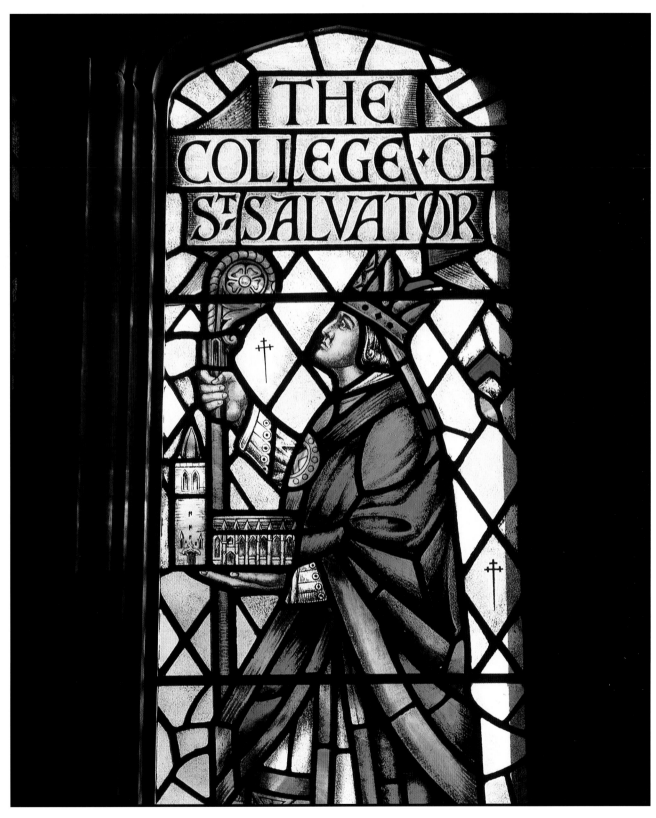

Bishop James Kennedy, founder of St Salvator's College, has a place in the dining-room in St Salvator's Hall, though his mind seems to be on higher matters than the menu.

Butts Wynd, so-called because it led from the burgh to the Bow Butts at the west end of the Scores where archery was once practised by all men and boys from 12 years upwards, by demand of the monarch, for national defence as well as sport. It is said that Mary Queen of Scots as well as the Marquis of Montrose both drew the bow at the Butts.

The interior of St Salvator's Chapel, a rare and beautiful example of late Gothic architecture, founded in 1450 as a part of Bishop James Kennedy's College of the Holy Saviour. The Chapel is well used during term time, with a Sunday service, daily prayers and occasional Evensong. Student groups also use the building for concerts and lunchtime recitals.

Alumni of the University of St Andrews from all over the world choose to return to take their vows in St Salvator's Chapel.

Herbert Hendrie (1887 – 1947), who taught at Edinburgh College of Art, is another major stained glass artist who has enhanced St Salvator's Chapel. The detail from his three-light window depicts the martyrdom of Patrick Hamilton, burned outside the chapel on 29th February 1528. The face raised to heaven in the flames expresses the agony and ecstasy of the first martyr of the Scottish Reformation.

St Mary's College

Step through the archway from South Street, and you are back in time among venerable buildings and white doves. The College of the Assumption of the Blessed Virgin Mary was founded in 1538 by Archbishop James Beaton as a bastion of Catholicism. The 'New College,' as it was known, was dedicated to a revival of learning on the Continental trilingual model, and from the outset laid emphasis on the knowledge of Latin, Greek and Hebrew. It received a re-foundation charter from Archbishop John Hamilton of St Andrews in 1553-4.

In the Reformation, while the altars of the Cathedral were strewn in ruins, the buildings of St Mary's were spared, to become the chief centre of Protestant teaching in Scotland. A school of Theology with five professors, including one of Hebrew, was established when, in 1579, St Mary's College was reconstituted as the Theological College of the University. Andrew Melville was appointed first Principal of St Mary's in 1580. Melville, who opposed the establishment of episcopacy in Scotland, is reputed to have described James VI and 1 to his face as 'God's silly vassal.'

The College survived through the turbulent times of the 17th century. A major rebuilding programme under Principal Robert Howie in the 1620s removed the ruinous old Hall, and created a new one in the old west building. Around this time a commission visited St Mary's College to reform 'the abuses thairin,' and commissioners appointed by the Covenanters visited in 1643. Samuel Rutherfurd was Principal of the New College and a leading Covenanter and churchman during the 1640s-50s, but was deprived of his position at the restoration of the monarch and episcopacy in 1660.

Only the northern and western blocks of the 16th century foundation survive, and help to form the suntrap that St Mary's College becomes on a summer's day. On the lawn beside the College's west range a large corniced sundial survives from 1664, casting its shadow over the turbulent times of the Covenant. On 3rd May 1679 Archbishop James Sharp, Chancellor of the University of St Andrews, was dragged from his coach and stabbed to death by a band of Covenanters near St Andrews.

Despite these turbulent events, St Mary's has endured and remains the home of the University's School of Divinity, now sharing its site with Psychology and Bio-Medical Science.

'In the beginning was the Word': the genesis of teaching in St Mary's College.

St Mary's College, sanctuary of doves and divines.

On a visit to St Mary's, his old college, during his Moderatorship of the General Assembly of the Church of Scotland, the Very Reverend Professor Robin Barbour was visited by the dove of peace. He was accompanied by the Very Reverend Professor James Whyte, Principal of St Mary's from 1978 to 1982. The third figure is the genial Dr Steven Watson, Principal of the University of St Andrews from 1966 to 1986, the year of his untimely death.

Was it in this tower of the Old Union Building that James Crichton lodged as a student when he went up to the University of St Andrews at the age of ten in 1571, astonishing his tutors, and later, Parisian society, by his teenage wisdom and facility in learning languages? However, his lethal skill as a swordsman could not save him from death at the age of 22 in a Mantua alleyway. A plaque on the wall of the building, considerably altered after his time, commemorates the 'Admirable Crichton.'

The central building of the three on South Street is St John's House, so named because it was once in the possession of the Knights of the Hospital of St John in Jerusalem, those crusaders against the infidel. The first house on the site was constructed of timber. St John's House and adjacent buildings are now occupied by the University's Medieval History Department, which has a distinguished reputation.

The vaulted understorey of Deans Court, now a dining-room, where the talk is peaceful and informed in a house which must have witnessed the fury of the Reformation across the way in the Cathedral.

Driving or walking about St Andrews, who can miss the Roundel on the busy bend at the end of South Street? Informed opinion is divided about its date of construction: probably 16th century, with the five bay fenestration remodelled a century or so later. But plain facts can't detract from its appeal and endurance.

In the grounds of St Mary's College, the building on the left is the addition to the Old Library, 1889-90, designed by W.W.Robertson in Scottish 17th century revival style, and clearly intended to reflect the genuine 17th century west wing of the College. The steel tycoon Andrew Carnegie donated £10,000 'to build a new library for beloved St Andrews,' and the classical building on the right, named after its benefactor, was designed by Robert Lorimer in 1906-09.

Linda Cannon's stained glass window of University Hall, St Andrews, executed in 1994, will evoke many happy memories for generations of female students who resided in the Hall during their studies. The newly-built Hall, the first for women students in Scotland, and the first residence for either men or women in St Andrews, was opened in 1896, under the Wardenship of the formidable Louisa Lumsden (created a Dame, 1935), one of the chief founders of St Leonards School in 1877, and its first headmistress. At the outbreak of the First World War the Hall became a military hospital for a brief time, but without receiving any casualties. The students planted potatoes and kept poultry in the Hall grounds, to help to feed themselves, the surplus going for the war effort. In the Second World War the residents shivered round their severely rationed coal fires while observing the blackout. In July and August each year the Hall becomes the much-loved home of the Royal Scottish Country Dance Society's Summer School. Lorna Walker was Warden of the Hall from 1961 to 1991, and her fascinating illustrated book *Celebrating a Centenary: University Hall 1896-1996*, recalls a happy home-from-home of dances, tea circles round the fire, and well-behaved male visitors. 'Hall,' as it was always known, is now a mixed residence.

The adaptation of buildings in St Andrews: the house on the left between Butts Wynd and the University Library was converted into a students' union by the Victorian architect Robert Rowand Anderson, who added a dining hall extension on the left. The building (left) now houses the complexities of Information Technology services, the extension the Research and Grants Finance Office.

Students rehearse in the University's elegant Younger Hall, scene of graduations and social occasions, with a dance floor reputed to be one of the finest in Scotland.

The Gateway at the North Haugh was a controversial building when it was erected in 2000, but has been accepted as an important addition to the architecture of St Andrews. Now owned by the University of St Andrews, the Gateway has a wide range of the most modern facilities. The café on the ground floor is open to the public, and the main meeting room can seat 200 delegates. There is space for art and other exhibitions. The University's School of Management occupies the two top floors.

University Rector

The first Rector of the University of St Andrews was the philosopher Laurence of Lindores (c.1372-1438), who had the ominous title Inquisitor of Heretical Pravity in Scotland, meaning that he rooted out heretics, and helped to send some to the stake. As Rector, Laurence's duties were the supervision and discipline of the University's general congregations. He also acted as a debt collector for the University.

Down the years the conditions governing the election of the Rector changed. After 1475 the students were excluded from casting their votes, a privilege restored in 1625, but lost again after 1642, when the Professors of Divinity decided who was to be Rector.

In the mid Victorian period the Rector lost his power over the University's affairs, and was elected every three years instead of annually. Politicians began to be elected as Rector, but too often did little or nothing for the University. However, when the 3rd Marquis of Bute was elected Rector in 1892, he was 'determined that the Rector should once more be the dominant figure in the university,' as the late Dr Ronald Cant, the University's eloquent historian, recorded.

Soldiers, statesmen and writers have been Rectors of the University of St Andrews. Sir James Barrie, author of 'Peter Pan,' gave a moving address on Courage when he was made Rector in 1922. Fridtof Nansen the polar explorer stressed the importance of the individual journey when he addressed the students of St Andrews in his 1926 Rectorial address: 'I am convinced that the future development of the possibilities of your own people, as well as those of mankind, will depend on some of you young people striking boldly out along new tracks.'

The modern Rector is elected by the students, and chairs the University Court. Figures from the media are favourite candidates. John Cleese of 'Fawlty Towers' fame was a popular choice as Rector, and the journalist Katharine Whitehorn was elected first woman Rector in 1982.

The custom at St Andrews has been to welcome the new Rector at the West Port, the city's ancient gateway, and having delivered an address in Latin, to haul him or her through the streets in a coach pulled by muscular students. Afterwards tradition gives way to informality, with a drink in the Union to welcome the new Rector.

Confab in the cloisters at the University of St Andrews: left to right – Ben Nicholson, the Rector's Assessor; the environmentalist Simon Pepper OBE, Rector; Tom d'Ardenne, President of the Students' Association; Laura Wilson, Director of Representation.

Two students at entrance to St Salvator's Quadrangle.

A light-box illuminates the history of painting for a first year Art History student. The University of St Andrews runs one of the most acclaimed Art History departments in the country, located in the splendid mansion which used to be the Principal's residence, and from whose large windows vistas of the North Sea help to explain perspective in painting.

Students play their cards right during Raisin Weekend, which is based on the tradition of academic 'families' at St Andrews. Third or fourth year students volunteer to act as 'parents' to interested first year students, introducing their 'children' to academic and social life in St Andrews. First year students traditionally present their 'parents' with a bottle of wine (formerly a pound of raisins), for which they receive a receipt written in Latin. It can be a messy exchange in St Salvator's Quadrangle.

The Harbour Walk is a Sunday morning tradition among St Andrews students, a way of clearing the head for the next week's studies, as well as a colourful occasion of scarlet gowns. It is said that in protest after women were admitted to the University, male students threw their mortar boards into the sea on the Harbour Walk, and never wore them again. Surely they were not so discourteous and shortsighted, considering how females have enhanced the academic - and social - life in all our universities.

Graduations

On attaining to his mastership at the medieval University of St Andrews a student was expected to present gloves and a birreta, or cap, to his teachers, and to provide a sumptuous banquet, presumably involving copious amounts of liquid refreshment. Nowadays, the extent of a graduating student's appreciation is to give a favourite teacher a bottle of wine, or treat him or her to a cup of coffee in a local café.

Some students weren't worried about their degrees. The Marquis of Montrose, at St Salvator's College between 1627 and 1629, spent much of his time on the Links, with a golf club, or at the butts with his bow, winning the Silver Arrow in 1628. But students of today have debts, not inherited wealth, so it's important to take a good degree, which is why the Library's lights burn late into the night before the Finals, when there is barely time for a carry-out, never mind a banquet.

Graduation is a colourful ceremony at St Andrews. Teachers and graduands are attired in their robes and colours, and the University's maces are processed. The generosity of the Younger family of Mount Melville provided the University with the Art Deco classical hall on North Street for graduations and other occasions, with the proud parents up on the balcony as the student kneels to the Chancellor. At the graduation ball in the marquee erected on one of St Salvator's lawns, kilt brogues pound the boards, and gowns swirl in reels.

Not only does the University honour its students: it also confers degrees on those from all over the world who have distinguished themselves in science and the arts. In 1759 Benjamin Franklin was awarded an honorary degree of L.L.D. in absentia.

But sportsmen also receive recognition from the University. Jack Nicklaus, winner of the 1970 Open Championship at St Andrews, one of the most thrilling in living memory, was an immensely popular graduate.

Nobel laureates are not uncommon in St Andrews in the graduation season, posing for photographs in the St Salvator's Quadrangle with their scrolls, with women as well as men honoured in a University that used to be strictly all-male.

Honorary graduates of the University of St Andrews: (top) The Dalai Lama is congratulated by Dr Frank Quinault of the University; (bottom) Mohammad Khatami, President of Iran between 1997 and 2005.

As if graduations at the University of St Andrews weren't glamorous enough already, the summer of 2006 was made even more memorable when Michael Douglas brought along his beautiful spouse Catherine Zeta-Jones to witness his award of an honorary degree, for his first class skills as an actor.

Visiting the University of St Andrews in the summer of 1982, Her Majesty the Queen was given a replica of the famous red gown to hand over to her grandson William. It must have impressed the Prince, because he decided to study at St Andrews.

(Opposite page): In the summer of 2005 his grandmother saw him capped by Sir Kenneth Dover, the then Chancellor of the University of St Andrews, with Jim Douglas the bedellus holding the hood.

A proud grandmother is the first to congratulate her grandson.

(Opposite page): Future kings - HRH Prince Charles and his wife Camilla, Duchess of Cornwall, came to St Andrews to see Prince William graduate.

Principal and Vice-Chancellor Dr Brian Lang shows his monarch the verdant attractions of the University of St Andrews while a dutiful and clearly happy Duke of Edinburgh follows.

The 3rd Marquis of Bute, Lord Rector of the University of St Andrews and philanthropist, wanted to make St Andrews a 'complete' University, with instruction in Medicine and Law as well as in Arts and Theology. To this end he paid for the impressive Bute Medical School, built between 1897 and 1899. A tower was intended, but never built. However, these students are happy in their environment.

The Kate Kennedy Club

In the late spring a motley procession on foot and horseback emerges from the archway of St Salvator's College and proceeds round the centre of St Andrews, applauded by the crowds lining the streets. You can nod to some of the most important personalities in the city's history as they pass you by.

The Kate Kennedy Club, organiser of the procession, takes its name from Kate, niece of Bishop James Kennedy, Bishop-Chancellor of the University, who founded St Salvator's College, and was one of the University's greatest academic statesmen.

There are those who like to believe that the Kate Kennedy Procession is a continuation of a medieval pageant, but most authorities concur with Dr Ronald Cant, the University's historian, that 'it would seem to have originated in 1849 as an end-of-the-session "rag" of the final year students in Arts.'

Believing that the procession brought disrepute on their institution, the University authorities suppressed it in the 1870s-80s. It was revived as a form of historical pageant in 1926.

The Kate Kennedy Club which mounts the pageant was formed in 1926 by two students (James Doak and Donald Kennedy) who were inspired by Sir James Barrie's Rectorial address on Courage that same year. The Kate Kennedy Club's aims are to: maintain the traditions of the University and town of St. Andrews; uphold and improve Town and Gown relations; and to raise money for local charities.

The Kate Kennedy Club website warns: 'The number of members cannot exceed sixty and only male matriculated students of the University of St Andrews are eligible to apply for membership. The Club admits nine bejants each year, after a series of interviews. It also invites male tertians and magistrands who the Club deems to have been outstanding contributors to the University, Town and Kate Kennedy Club to join.'

Kate is represented by a male student in drag, a coveted role as 'she' is driven through St Andrews in a coach in the company of her uncle the Bishop.

The saintly 11th century Queen Margaret of Scotland steps out in the Kate Kennedy Procession. The chief authority for Margaret's life is the contemporary biography ascribed to Turgot, the Saint's confessor, a monk of Durham and later Archbishop of St Andrews. Margaret arranged a crossing on the Forth (Queensferry) to bring pilgrims across to the shrine of St Andrew.

The University's Collections

As one would expect from Scotland's oldest university, St Andrews has an outstanding collection of artefacts dating back to its inception, some educational, some recreational. The 'black stone' on which students sat for their oral examinations has been preserved, along with the medals from the annual 'Silver Arrow' archery competition from 1618 to 1754. There are about 12,000 pieces in the University's collection of Scottish Communion tokens.

Some of Scotland's finest silver, furniture and fine art are housed around the University. Through the Museum Collections it is possible to trace the changing life of the University, its place in Scottish history and its role in the history of education.

Over the centuries the University has also been accumulating items of material culture from overseas, such as a Hindu sculpture associated with the invention of the rubber golf ball, because it was supposed to have been packed in gutta percha. Ladislav Holy, Professor of Social Anthropology at St Andrews from 1987 to 1997, bequeathed a number of African items to the collections, including a diviner's wand which belonged to a Toka tribesman from the Kaloma district of Zambia.

The furniture collections include many fine pieces, mainly of Scottish workmanship, from the 16th to the 20th centuries. A particular highlight is a set of Knibb Clocks purchased by the University in 1673. In July 1673 Professor James Gregory wrote: 'I have two pendulum clocks makinge with long swinges, vibratinge seconds, and pointinge houres, minits and seconds, without striking; and also one little pendulum clock vibrating 4 times in a second.' These were the two long case clocks and the split seconds clock.

A 17th century ceremonial armchair is, according to tradition, the one used by the presiding officer when the Scottish Parliament sat in the University's 'Public School' (since renamed 'Parliament Hall') in 1645-6.

The Library of the University of St Andrews holds one of the largest and most important collections of historic photography in Scotland, in excess of 300,000 images, and still being increased by acquisition. The images exist in a wide variety of formats: negative (on glass and film of varying sizes), lantern slides, prints (from salt paper to modern photographic), postcards and modern transparencies.

The mace of the Faculty of Arts, of silver, partly gilt, was commissioned in 1414-15 and completed by 1418-19. The hexagonal head of gothic tabernacle work is arranged in three ascending and slightly receding stages, the lower stage with an angel on each face. The next stage consists of six panels engraved with the likenesses of saints, including Andrew, and also the Virgin and Child.

A page from the 'St Andrews Psalter,' showing the initial of Psalm 80. The initial letters of Psalms 1, 26, 38, 52, 68, 80, 97, and 109 are superbly illuminated in colour and gold-leaf, with foliage and animals. In addition, the initial of Psalm One contains a miniature of King David. The manuscript and rare book collections of the University of St Andrews represent over five centuries of scholarship and learning in a huge diversity of subjects.

This Universal Instrument from the University Museum Collections was made in London in 1582 by Humphrey Cole, the most important scientific instrument maker of the Elizabethan age. Believed to be the only such instrument still in existence, it allows the celestial co-ordinates of a heavenly body to be determined.

The ruins of St Andrews Cathedral as featured in the photography of the Victorian pioneers of the art, David Octavius Hill and Robert Adamson. The development of photography was a collaboration between Sir David Brewster, Principal of the United College, William Henry Fox Talbot, the English inventor of the calotype photographic process, and Dr John Adamson, the brother of Robert. In May 1840 Dr Adamson produced the first calotype taken in Scotland. Robert shared his brother's interest in the new art form, and went into partnership with the painter David Octavius Hill. Their photographs of St Andrews are precious historical records.

This isn't an early example of an alarm clock, to rouse sleepy St Andrews students, but a special chronological instrument that has numbered pegs to determine when the bell will ring. Used in psychology experiments, it is preserved in the University Museum Collections.

Mary Queen of Scots

The arrival of Mary Queen of Scots in St Andrews on Sunday 21st September 1561 as part of a royal progress must have been a memorable day for the citizens, a sad day for her. Two years previously the reformers had descended on the Cathedral 'to purge the kirk and break down the altars and images and all kind of idolatrie...'

The Catholic Mary must have averted her eyes from the destruction, because her mother, Mary of Guise, had been married in St Andrews Cathedral in 1538. But Mary Queen of Scots must also have been apprehensive that Sabbath of her 1561 visit to St Andrews, since agents of her great adversary John Knox were evidently mingling with the crowds. It has been claimed that a priest was assassinated that day in St Andrews, a reminder to Mary of Protestant domination of the religion that was at the centre of her life.

On that visit Mary might have stayed with her half-brother the Lord James Stewart, Commendator of St Andrews Priory. But on her later visits to St Andrews she stayed in the new house which Alan Meldrum, Vicar of Leuchars and Canon of the Priory, built for himself in 1525.

This residence, known appropriately as St Mary's House, is part of St Leonards School on South Street in the shadow of the Cathedral's ruins. On her holiday in St Andrews in 1565 Mary played with her 'Four Maries' at being bourgeois women, and keeping house.

The Queen is believed to have been a number of times in St Andrews between 1561 and 1565, testifying to her love of the place, a haven from the problems of Edinburgh, and certainly healthier. In her billowing gowns of gold and silver, with embroideries and bordures, she must have looked like the modern equivalent of a film star as she trod the streets of St Andrews. Queen Mary's Thorn Tree (or perhaps its predecessor) in St Mary's College grounds is reputed to have been planted by her.

Mary's time in St Andrews is memorably detailed in My Heart is my Own, a new life of the tragic queen by acclaimed historian Professor John Guy, formerly of the University of St Andrews, and now a Fellow of Clare College, Cambridge.

Queen Mary's House from the grounds of St Leonards School, which converted the dwelling into a library in 1927, with further conversion fifty years later. Computers now click where, perhaps, Mary sighed over her embroidery as she pondered problems of state and of love.

'I was the Queen o' bonie France,
Where happy I hae been;
Fu' lightly raise I in the morn,
As blythe lay down at e'en:
And I'm the sov'reign of Scotland,
And mony a traitor there;
Yet here I lie in foreign bands,
And never-ending care.'
Robert Burns

St Andrews, Home of Golf

There seems to be more balls than birds in the air around St Andrews these days. Golf is the great allure. In 1123 King David granted the Links to the residents of St Andrews. The earliest written reference to golf dates to 1457, when King James II decreed a ban on golf and football.

The first document mentioning golf in St Andrews itself dates back to 1552. This deed, bearing the seal of Archbishop Hamilton, refers to the public ownership of the Links, which were used for golf, football, shooting and the grazing of livestock.

An 18th century minute states: 'The Noblemen and Gentlemen above named being admirers of the ancient and healthfull exercise of the golf and at the same time having the interest and prosperity of the ancient city of St Andrews at heart, being the Alma Mater of the golf, did in this year of our Lord 1754 contribute for a silver club having a St Andrews engraved on the head thereof, to be played for on the links of St Andrews upon the 14th day of May said year and yearly in time coming'. The first clear evidence that the 'Noblemen and Gentlemen' had formed themselves into a society can be found in a minute of 4th May 1766.

In 1834 the society's future was assured when King William 1V became its patron, conferring the title 'The Royal and Ancient Golf Club of St Andrews.' The R&A became the premier club, and in 1897 its first Rules of Golf Committee was appointed. In 1974 the St Andrews Links Trust was created by an Act of Parliament to continue running the Links as public golf courses open to anyone.

In 1990 the stylish British Golf Museum was built in St Andrews, a decent drive from the 18th green. The chronological display of clubs, balls and Open Medals, including the five won by J.H. Taylor and James Braid, and the innovative techniques used to bring the history of the game alive, will keep the enthusiast fascinated until the rain slackens and play resumes.

Old Tom Morris and Young Tom

He doesn't look like today's golfers in their smart garb, but Old Tom Morris would have given them a good game. Born in North Street in 1821, he was on the Links with a golf club from the age of six while other boys were whipping their iron hoops through the streets. Tom left Madras College to learn the art of making feathery golf balls from Alan Robertson in St Andrews before setting up his own ball-manufactory in the city.

Perhaps it didn't pay, because Tom went south to Prestwick, where he worked as a greenkeeper. But he returned to St Andrews, and was appointed greenkeeper and professional golfer to the Royal & Ancient in 1865. Immersed in all aspects of the game, Tom competed in every Open Championship from its inception in 1860, to 1896, winning it four times. Since he laid out the Old Course in its present form, it is fitting that the 18th hole is named after him. St Andrews mourned 'The Grand Old Man of Golf' when Tom died in 1908.

His son, known as Young Tom Morris, appears to have been born with a club in his hands. He lifted his first prize money at the age of 16, and went on to win the Open Championship Belt four times before he was 21.

Tragedy clouded Young Tom's golf career. Coming off the course at North Berwick, he was handed a telegram informing him that his wife had been taken ill during childbirth. On his way home, he received another telegram telling him that he was too late. The child also died, and the broken-hearted husband and father passed away a few months later on Christmas Day 1875. It must have been a day of mourning in St Andrews, where his character was as much admired as his prowess with a club.

The memorials to the legendary Morris father and son can be seen in the Cathedral cemetery. Sixty golfing societies contributed to Young Tom's tombstone, showing him wearing a tam o' shanter, and with a club in his hands.

This composite picture shows the plaque to the golfing legend Old Tom Morris on the wall of the Royal & Ancient Clubhouse, and the relief figure of Young Tom Morris on his tombstone in the Cathedral cemetery.

After his third consecutive Open Championship win Young Tom Morris was allowed to keep this belt.

(Opposite page): Local actor, writer, and artist David Joy has delighted thousands of people with his uncanny recreation of Old Tom Morris, golfer and gentleman.

Born in St Andrews in 1815, Allan Robertson earned his place among the golfing immortals by being the world's first professional golfer and the first player to break 80 at St Andrews – using a ball he made himself, one assumes. His gravestone in the Cathedral grounds is a place of pilgrimage for those who worship the game.

A craftsman continues the tradition of club making in St Andrews. In 1672 James Pett supplied the Marquis of Montrose with clubs. However, the noble Lord didn't lose his head on the Links, but on the scaffold. Heritage Golf specialises in making exact replicas of antique hickory-shafted clubs.

He looks isolated as he receives an honorary degree from the University of St Andrews. But Charlie Sifford is now welcomed wherever he goes. Considered to be the grandfather of African American golf, he was the first black man to win a PGA tour event, and devoted much of his career to challenging the golfing establishment for the right to compete on an equal basis with whites. Charlie Sifford's achievement as sportsman and civil rights activist is shown by the fact that he was the first black chosen for the World Golf Hall of Fame. It is surely fitting that he has been honoured in the Home of Golf.

St Andrews! They say that thy glories are gone,
That thy streets are deserted, thy castles o'erthrown.
If thy glories be gone, they are only, methinks,
As it were, by enchantment, transferred to thy links.

(Over page): Golf courses, and particularly the Old Course, need constant tending.
A computerised water system keeps the greens in form.

Perhaps the medieval Swilken Bridge over the burn which flows through the Old Course should be called the Bridge of Sighs, since so many disconsolate golfers must have crossed it, cursing their drives.

Peter Dawson, Chief Executive of The R & A, in the Big Room of the Clubhouse at St Andrews, no doubt hoping that the Captains of the past would approve of the Club's modern day activities. Looking down are former Captains, the Prince of Wales (later Edward V111), and John White Melville.

The Royal & Ancient members enjoy different kinds of rounds by night, where over a glass the day's play is discussed.

Are the clouds moving in from the North Sea going to force the abandonment of play on the Old Course, the most famous golfing links in the world, host to twenty six Open Championships to date?

A rainbow over the Royal & Ancient Clubhouse, as rare as a hole in one.

For the things we've said to our caddies, for the things we've said to the ball,
For the things we've said in bunker, for silence profaner than all,
We shall pay for them each twice over and again and again and again,
Puffing and panting, perspiring for ever and ever. Amen.

W.G. Strachan

(Opposite page): Spectacular pyrotechnics at the Dunhill Links Championship at St Andrews, established as a world-class golfing event.

The Architecture of St Andrews

The St Andrews you walk through today is very different from the city in the 1930s. Many of the small streets and wynds had deteriorated, and the Housing Act of 1930 meant that they were the target of the demolition hammer, irrespective of their historical or architectural importance.

In 1933 nearly 80 properties in St Andrews, including some in the heart of the old town, were scheduled to be demolished in a five year plan to rid the city of insanitary housing. Local criticism found an eloquent protester in Sir James Irvine, Principal of the University. On receiving the Freedom of the city in 1930, he declared that his 'prayer was that St Andrews be preserved before it was too late.'

Two people arrived in St Andrews in the mid 1930s who would take up Principal Irvine's call and do so much to preserve the character of the city. Ronald Cant was the University's first lecturer in Medieval History, and Miss Annabel Kidston was a gifted artist and teacher.

Mr Cant and Miss Kidston organised a public meeting in December 1937, from which was formed the St Andrews Preservation Trust in the following year. Its aim was 'to preserve, for the benefit of the public, the amenities and historic character of the City and Royal Burgh of St Andrews and its neighbourhood.'

The Trust lost its first battle with officialdom over the demolition of Baker Lane, one of the old wynds running between Market Street and South Street. But the Trust had learned how to deal with bureaucracy, and when Louden's Close, a classic example of a complete rigg or burgher tenement, was marked down for demolition, the Trust persuaded the local authority to let it take on the reconstruction of the buildings in bad repair in the Close. The money came from the Pilgrim Trust, and Louden's Close and its frontage on 146-148 South Street were saved.

The St Andrews Preservation Trust developed its innovative policy of restoring old properties and using the proceeds to fund further preservation schemes. One of its most important purchases was the old fisherman's cottage in North Street, which, though not restored by the Trust itself, has been turned into a Museum.

Raindrops bead railings at St Andrews Cathedral in this atmospheric view along North Street.

(Over page): 'Its series of great medieval buildings and its characteristic domestic architecture of the 16th 17th and early 18th century...are in fact without serious rival in Scotland unless it be the old town of Edinburgh. It is also remarkably well endowed with fine buildings of the next architectural period [Georgian and early Victorian]...' Dr Ronald Cant, doyen of historians of St Andrews and benefactor to the city, some of whose historic buildings he helped to save, wrote these words. The kenspeckle historian and raconteur, much missed in St Andrews, bequeathed his house in Kinburn Place, together with capital and his extensive library to form the Strathmartine Trust, to advance the study of Scottish history and to give scholars congenial surroundings in which to pursue their interests.

At the centre of the city, Holy Trinity Church. In 1634, Charles the First, having visited St Andrews the previous year, was determined to have the church so 'ordored' that 'the fabrick may, according to the first lawdable intention of the founder, appear in the trew forme and proportion thairof, without being anywayes parcelled or pestred within in the beautie of the walls, or lights obscured without.' Since this royal decree the fabric of Holy Trinity has undergone many alterations. The demolition of the old church began early in June 1907, and the new one was opened in November 1909. Portions of the carved woodwork from the old church disappeared into houses in St Andrews.

Bird's eye perspective: from the Old Course, to the newest one, Fairmont St Andrews, top centre.

At this end of North Street the fisher folk used to sit on the steps of their houses, baiting hooks or unravelling nets as barefooted children trundled their iron girds (hoops).

The Roundel (right) and the remains of an ancient wall flank the entrance to South Street, with the spire of Holy Trinity Church (left), and rolling farmyard beyond.

Kings and commoners have ridden, and then driven through the West Port, the main approach to the city. Stone from the earlier gate was recycled when the West Port was erected in 1589 by a local mason, using Edinburgh's Netherbow Port as the model. But the West Port has its own character, and a modern use as a traffic calmer.

The old and the apparently old in harmony. The spire of Holy Trinity Church shares the skyline with the premises of J.G. Innes. After John Innes purchased the property of the printer Robert Tullis, it was reconstructed as the offices of the St Andrews Citizen by local architects Walker & Pride in 1932, and is one of the most intriguing buildings in St Andrews.

(Over page): Up to twenty fisher folk used to crowd into this 17th century house at 12-16 North Street. Restored by local architect James H. Scott in the 1930s, the building was purchased in the 1960s by St Andrews Preservation Trust and is now its museum, an essential visit for locals and tourists, with the city's history recreated through artifacts and photographs.

Many senior citizens of St Andrews remember this elegant jar in Keith's the Chemist, now dispensing again in the Preservation Trust Museum. But the chilblain cure is no longer available.

For the sake of perspective, another precarious vantage-point for the photographer. In the foreground, the chimneys of St Leonards School, with St Leonard's Chapel and the ruined Cathedral beyond.

In charming College Street, with its Georgian houses and lack of traffic, are these two students making a date, or discussing a lecture on the Romantic Poets?

Has anyone seen the ghost of a fishwife sitting on these stairs, baiting lines on a summer's day? Joan's House in South Castle Street would have been reduced to rubble by the demolition hammer, had it not been for the vision of the St Andrews Preservation Trust, which purchased the property in 1939. The former hovel has been restored and is now a most desirable residence.

Another glimpse into the past of St Andrews down Louden's Close, which faced demolition in the late 1930s, but was saved by the St Andrews Preservation Trust in 1939, with several of the houses restored in the 1940s. Their sale carried conditions obliging the owners to preserve their architectural character.

After the amalgamation of St Leonard's and St Salvator's Colleges in the United College, in 1772 the main St Leonard's site, with the college buildings, was sold to Professor Robert Watson for £200, surely the bargain of a lifetime. The house with the bow window was the home of Sir Hugh Lyon Playfair, who retired from active military service in 1834, and became Provost of St Andrews. The building on the extreme right between the walls was the residence of Sir David Brewster, philosopher, writer, and scientist, Principal of the United Colleges of the University from 1838 to 1859, and inventor of the kaleidoscope in 1816.

Sir Hugh Lyon Playfair, Provost of St Andrews from 1842 until his death in 1861, is credited with modernising the city, but at the same time removing some of its ancient character. The momorial fountain to him on the Scores is by Robert Lorimer. The great Edwardian architect was clearly a dog lover, for there is provision for our canine companions to drink from the fountain, as well as their owners. The old Grand Hotel, which became Hamilton Hall, a University residence, has been sold and is being transformed into timeshare apartments in which the seriously rich can sit overlooking the 18th Hole with their glasses of champagne to toast the winner of the Open Championship.

You could easily miss Rose Lane on your stroll along South Street. Pantiled houses, a small 18th century brewery at the foot; a place of shade and peace a few paces away from the centre of the city.

Castellated Kinburn House was built in the mid 19th century on land purchased by Dr David Buddo of the Indian Medical Service. The name sounds local, but was taken from a Russian fort captured during the Crimean War. St Andrews Town Council acquired Kinburn House in 1920. It was opened as a museum in 1991, and is well worth a visit.

South Court must have ranked among the most desirable local authority housing in Scotland. This town mansion, with the date 1646 on its title-deeds, was built by a Provost of St Andrews, and lay derelict at the beginning of the 20th century until the Town Council reconstructed it, allocating the flats on a temporary basis to those in need of housing. Major renovation in 1968-72 created flats of character.

On Open Doors day each year one of the modern artistic treasures of St Andrews can be visited, through a narrow alley and up unprepossessing stone stairs. Lodge St Andrew No 25 has occupied part of the Town Hall ever since it was built in 1858-62. Having contributed generously to the public subscription for the building's erection, the Lodge members were granted the right to meet there in perpetuity – a right they also enjoyed in the old Town Hall in Market Street. The Lodge's Brethren first met in the Town Chambers, but then moved upstairs in 1898, paying for the conversion of the empty attic out of their own funds. Visitors are awestruck by the magnificent ceiling embellishment in the elegant attic chamber. The painting within the dome was the labour of love of the Dundee artist George Wilkie Gahan a century ago, and depicts Masonry in various classic sites throughout the world. As the above photograph shows, the ruins of St Andrews Cathedral are featured because the tradition in the Lodge is that it was founded by the operative masons engaged in building the Cathedral. Also in the photograph is St Mark's, Venice.

The elegant sweep of Howard Place. Georgian survival; highly desirable. The picture was taken from the University's McIntosh Hall in Abbotsford Crescent where, as a plaque records outside number 8, the late Jo Grimond, Leader of the Liberal Party, was born into the comfort of a jute family fortune in 1913.

The Central, Market Street, a favourite howff for students, citizens and visitors. There have been licensed premises on the site since 1887.

Ceiling detail from the Town Hall, at the junction of South Street and Queen's Gardens. Baronial with a Flemish flavour, the Hall has served St Andrews for a century and a half.

Shopna Farhad is a charming member of staff in the Balaka Bangladeshi Restaurant in Alexandra Place, which was established in 1981, and is famous for its herb garden as well as its food.

(Over page): The name Rufflets is said to derive from old Scots, 'Ruch (pronounced ruff) Flets,' meaning 'rough, flat lands,' when the land was owned by the Priory of St Andrews. The mansion was built in 1924 as a private home for Mrs Anne Brydon Gilroy, the widow of a prominent Dundee jute baron, and designed by the well-known Dundee architect, Donald Mills. The house has been privately owned and managed by three generations of the same family since 1952, and is one of Scotland's finest hotels.

Don & Nancy Panoz, founders of Château Élan Hotels & Resorts, had a vision on a cliff-top location along the coast from St Andrews: an international resort overlooking the Home of Golf. St Andrews Bay opened in the summer of 2001. The hotel, now under new ownership and renamed Fairmont St Andrews, is airy and spacious, the environment busy with birds and golf balls.

Silver and paintings from another era await the connoisseur in David Brown's antiques shop in Albany Place, a house with the date 1809 on the wall, converted to a treasure trove.

This interior in fashionable Greyfriars Garden used to be a book and print shop. Now scissors snip and clients chat in Sophie Butler's, among the frowning shades of scholars raising their heads from tomes.

This could be a window in St Andrews of the past, before the age of modernisation and expansion.

Searching for a good read at the stall by the fountain in Market Street where plants are sold, and preachers warn passers-by of the error of their ways.

Farmore Interiors of South Street offers a decoration service for the discerning in an interior which preserves the elegance of a past age.

Gordon Casely led the colourful parade when the 27th International Congress of Genealogical and Heraldic Sciences came to St Andrews in the summer of 2006. The Congress was declared an outstanding success by participants and citizens.

The City of St Andrews Pipe Band was formed in 1972, out of the Boys' Brigade ex members pipe band. By effort and talent it has risen from Grade 4 to Grade 2 status, and competes in the annual World Pipe Band Championships in Glasgow. The band's tartan is red Erskine, and its stirring pipes and drums entertain locals and visitors for special events in the streets of St Andrews.

Schools in St Andrews

St Andrews is well served by schools, both state and private. Madras College's name derives from the system of education devised by the school's founder, the Rev. Dr. Andrew Bell. Born in St. Andrews in 1753, the son of a local magistrate and wig-maker, he studied mathematics at the University. Dr Bell was a tutor to a prominent plantation family in Virginia, but his Loyalist sympathies forced him to return to Britain on the outbreak of the American War of Independence.

Becoming a Church of England clergyman, he became chaplain to the regiments of the East India Company in Madras, where his duties included the education of the soldiers' children. Due to the shortage of teachers, he used the older boys, who had been taught the lesson by the master, to instruct the younger pupils. This is the basis of 'the Madras system,' the name given to the St Andrews school off South Street which he founded from his fortune. Work began on his magnificent legacy in 1832, the year of his death, and left St Andrews with one of its finest buildings. The large modern additions are 'mercifully well hidden at the back,' according to the architectural historian John Gifford when he surveyed Fife for the Buildings of Scotland series.

St Leonards is another famous school in St Andrews. It was founded in 1877 as an all-girls school, with Dame Louisa Lumsden, that great champion of women's emancipation, as its headmistress.

St Leonards School moved to its present site – the University's St Leonard's College – in 1882. Behind its high walls is one of the most attractive campuses in Britain, with a range of buildings spanning over three centuries and including an inspirational Music School built by Morris & Steedman in 1986. St Leonards, which amalgamated with New Park, the independent preparatory school formerly located in Hepburn Gardens, is now co-educational, taking in boys and girls from 3 to 19 years of age. Its successful Sixth Form College offers the International Baccalaureate to students from all over the world.

Relaxed learning at Canongate Primary School, St Andrews. The school has merged with Langlands Primary on the Canongate site, and Greyfriars Roman Catholic Primary is to move into the Langlands school from the site that it has occupied since 1889.

An outdoor art class at Madras College, designed by William Burn in the Jacobean style, using Dr Bell's generous legacy. The main buildings, as grand as any state school in the land, stand behind lawns off South Street.

In the leafy concealed campus of St Leonards School the youngest student looks up to the oldest, though height isn't always an advantage.

The Byre Theatre

Alexander B Paterson, local freelance journalist and prolific playwright, had a dream as he walked the streets of St Andrews between the Wars. The expanding city with its University and wide cultural interests deserved a theatre. But where, Paterson pondered as he searched for a suitable location in the streets and wynds.

He saw the possibility in the old byre in the Abbey Street Dairy Farm. After being cleaned up to make it fit for human habitation the cowshed opened its doors in 1933, with the cast coming from a theatre group from Hope Park Church. Alex Paterson and others formed the St. Andrews Play Club to take on the lease of the new theatre from the Council.

In the beginning the invited audience squatted on cushions on the floor, but within a couple of years the byre was crowded out as word spread about the polished performances. However, in 1935 officialdom stepped in, insisting that the theatre upgrade its facilities to enable a licence for public performances to be granted. The first performance in the newly licensed theatre was in May 1937.

The theatre kept going throughout the dark days and nights of the war, thanks to the St Andrews Repertory Company, when it was important to bring some diversion to the city.

In 1969 the original cowshed that had become a theatrical legend was demolished to make way for a housing development. With the support of funds raised by a public appeal and the local authority, a new theatre was opened in 1970. The first performance in the new building was Weir of Hermiston, written by Alex Paterson himself.

Ambitious plays were brought to St Andrews. In 1982 capacity audiences sat sad but enthralled through the Diary of Anne Frank.

Alex Paterson died in 1989, when the expansion of the theatre's facilities was under active discussion. It's said that some theatres are haunted. Does Alex Paterson's delighted ghost appear in the magnificent new Byre Theatre, built by award winning architects Nicoll Russell Studios of Broughty Ferry, a stone and glass monument to the founder, as well as one of the best equipped theatres in Britain? The programmes are ambitious and varied, from hilarious contemporary comedies to heavyweight Shakespeare. If 'all the world's a stage,' the Byre Theatre becomes the Globe.

A view of the Byre Theatre the public don't see. It was taken from the roof of St Leonards School.

The Twits, Roald Dahl's hilarious creation, almost brought down the roof of the Byre Theatre. Philip Scutt is performing the handstand, held up by Jimmy Johnston. Garry Lake lounges on the roof.

Patrick Barlow's adaptation of John Buchan's classic The 39 Steps (top) was a resounding success when it was produced by the Byre Theatre. Gail Watson (back left), Hugh Parker (back right), Graham Cramond (front left) and Peter Kelly (front right) kept up the fast pace.

The revered memory of A.B. Paterson, begetter of the Byre Theatre, was carried forward with the revival of his comedy The Open, with (left to right), Brenda Hunter, Heidi Nicholson and Sandra Skeldon.

Lammas Market

On the second Monday and Tuesday in August the oldest surviving medieval market in Scotland comes to St Andrews, the stalls and attractions hauled, not by horses, but by engine power.

The word Lammas derives from Lunasdal, the Celtic festival of autumn at which the fruits of the soil were honoured. It was King James V1 and 1 who in 1620 granted the burghers of St Andrews the right to hold a Lammas Market, a privilege confirmed by an Act of Parliament in the reign of Charles 1.

St Andrews was one of five fairs, or holy days, with merchants arriving from across the North Sea to do business in St Andrews. The Market later served an important function as a feeing, or hiring market for farm servants, a process discontinued with the advent of the First World War.

Where once a ploughman was committed to a local farm by a handshake, vendors hold out soft toys, and invitations to try one's luck at the stalls, where the ring never seems to go over the block with the glittering prize resting on it.

The cobbles of Market Street vibrate with the throb of the dodgems, with the attendants leaping like Hollywood stunt-men between the moving cars in order to collect the fares. A pneumatic arm hoists shrieking children on the wheel into the evening sky above St Andrews.

The Lammas Fair may be an anachronism to many, but it is still a time of business for the stall-holders, since they have to pay for their stances.

Critics complain that the benefits which the Lammas Fair brings to St Andrews are lost through the traffic congestion caused at the height of the tourist season, and it has been suggested that the Fair be relocated to the West Sands. But it would be a pity if this survival of medieval ritual was to be removed from St Andrews, because of the excitement it engenders among young and old, with grandparents nibbling on sticks of sherbet which remind them of their younger days.

Magnificently attired, Fabien Troivaux from France dances the Highland Fling in the ruins of St Andrews Castle, accompanied by Lauren Galloway. A graduate of the University of St Andrews and a member of its old established Celtic Society, Fabien's love of Scottish dancing demonstrates the international scope of its appeal. St Andrews can claim to be the home of dancing in Scotland, since the Royal Scottish Country Dance Society (founded 1923), held its first Summer School in St Andrews in 1927. Since then, tens of thousands of dancers from all over the world have congregated in July and August each year to learn new dances, improve their technique, and fraternise with old friends. Lauren, the elegant and talented young piper providing the reel, is a member of Madras College Pipe Band and wears the Band's tartan.

Botanic Garden

The shaded trees and superb blooms of the St Andrews Botanic Garden make it feel as if it has been on the same site for a century. But it comes as a surprise to learn that the original Botanic Garden was founded by the University of St Andrews in 1889 in the precincts of St. Mary's College, by a group of enthusiasts led by Dr John Wilson. The original quarter acre garden consisted of 78 regularlyshaped beds laid out according to the Bentham and Hooker plant classification.

Gardens grow, and by 1960 the St Mary's garden covered nearly an acre, and with additional collections spread through the University campus. It was time to find a new site, and the present Botanic Garden of 18.5 acres was created from two fields between Hepburn Gardens and The Canongate in the early 1960s. Lovingly supervised by Curator Bob Mitchell, the Garden is now managed by Fife Council.

Several layers of plants were planned: from tall forest trees and small trees to large and small shrubs, to make full use of the space available and to grow plants in the conditions they would naturally inhabit.

As well as being an important botanical site with teaching and research functions, the St Andrews Botanic Garden is also a place of peace and fragrances where citizens and visitors can stroll and sit to have a picnic.

About 8000 species of ferns, herbaceous plants, shrubs and trees are grown in the Garden. Some are native to Scotland, but most grow wild in other regions of the world and can survive the bracing climate of the Fife coast. More delicate plants flourish in the glasshouses.

Worldwide contact with other specialist gardens is maintained, for example, through seed exchanges. The Garden is recognised and registered by the International Union for the Conservation of Nature, and botanical and horticultural research is carried out there.

Even if you cannot visit St Andrews, keying into the website at www.st-andrews-botanic.org which is maintained by the Friends of St Andrews Botanic Garden, will give you pleasure.

Lade Braes

A walk along the Lade Braes is a lesson in history as well as an aesthetic experience. The medieval Priory required power to turn its water wheels, so a 'lade' was cut, to take water from the Kinness Burn. After the Priory was wrecked in the Reformation, the lade continued to flow, turning the wheels of meal and other mills en route to the sea until the channel was filled in about 1860.

In the Victorian era the planters got to work, to provide shelter for St Andrews and environs against the salt-laden winds. Stretching through the town centre from east to west, the Lade Braes is a classic walk on a summer's day. The foliage shelters wildlife, and is a haunt of the photographer and the bird-watcher, who may catch the flash of a kingfisher. It is also a place to reflect on love, as the following poem shows.

I wander on the Lade Braes, where I used to walk with you,
And purple are the woods of Mount Melville, budding new,
But I cannot bear to look, for the tears keep coming so,
And the Spring has lost the freshness which it had a year ago.

Yet often I could fancy, where the pathway takes a turn,
I shall see you in a moment, coming round beside the burn,
Coming round beside the burn, with your swinging step and free,
And your face lit up with pleasure at the sudden sight of me.

R.F. Murray

Only a duck disturbs the reflection of a red pantiled roof on the Lade Braes walk.

Has she a tryst, or is she reflecting on the water of the Lade Braes?

Foliage on the Lade Braes shades the stone to John Milne, the visionary St Andrews councillor who had the Braes planted, and so gave succeeding generations so much pleasure.

The painstaking process of unearthing a skeleton in its stone cist on Hallow Hill, where the Kinness and Cairnsmill burns meet. This sacred site dates back as a burial ground to at least the late Roman and early Christian periods. Some 150 cists have been excavated, at least twenty in 1860, and the others during major excavations supervised by Mrs Edwina Proudfoot in the 1970s. A display board and a group of five cists can be visited, near the top of the hill, a pleasant walk, where visitors and local people can reflect on the antiquity of St Andrews.

St Andrews, 1862, Oxford, 1865

St. Andrews by the Northern sea,
A haunted town it is to me!
A little city, worn and grey,
The grey North Ocean girds it round.
And o'er the rocks, and up the bay,
The long sea-rollers surge and sound.
And still the thin and biting spray
Drives down the melancholy street,
And still endure, and still decay,
Towers that the salt winds vainly beat.
Ghost-like and shadowy they stand
Dim mirrored in the wet sea-sand.

St. Leonard's chapel, long ago
We loitered idly where the tall
Fresh budded mountain ashes blow
Within thy desecrated wall:
The tough roots rent the tomb below,
The April birds sang clamorous,
We did not dream, we could not know
How hardly Fate would deal with us!

O, broken minster, looking forth
Beyond the bay, above the town,
O, winter of the kindly North,
O, college of the scarlet gown,
And shining sands beside the sea,
And stretch of links beyond the sand,
Once more I watch you, and to me
It is as if I touched his hand!

Andrew Lang

The North Sea rolls on to the East Sands, spume on the camera lens creating a bracing effect in the high spring tide.

Where has it come from – Fife Ness, or a forest across in Denmark? It's a reminder of how ferocious and destructive the North Sea can be.

Against a glorious sunrise a solitary jogger paces the tide.

The road to St Andrews from the Grange, priory farmsteads where monks might have raked the harvest in centuries past.

The Promise

*While the earth remaineth
seedtime and harvest
and cold and heat
and summer and winter
and day shall not cease*

Genesis viii. 22.

A view of St Andrews which few travellers see nowadays. The gentle undulating countryside leads down from Wester Balrymouth, a way that pilgrims must have taken in the past.

Winter in St Andrews

The city once again doth wear
Her wonted dress of winter's bride,
Her mantle woven of misty air,
With saffron sunlight faintly dyed.
She sits above the seething tide,
Of all her summer robes forlorn -
And dead is all her summer pride -
The leaves are off Queen Mary's Thorn.

All round, the landscape stretches bare,
The bleak fields lying far and wide,
Monotonous, with here and there
A lone tree on a lone hillside.
No more the land is glorified
With golden gleams of ripening corn,
Scarce is a cheerful hue descried -
The leaves are off Queen Mary's Thorn.

For me, I do not greatly care
Though leaves be dead, and mists abide.
To me the place is thrice as fair
In winter as in summer-tide:
With kindlier memories allied
Of pleasure past and pain o'erworn.
What care I, though the earth may hide
The leaves from off Queen Mary's Thorn?

Thus I unto my friend replied,
When, on a chill late autumn morn,
He pointed to the tree, and cried,
`The leaves are off Queen Mary's Thorn!'

R.F. Murray

St Salvator's tower is one of the best known landmarks in St Andrews.

A solitary figure passes through snowfall in St Salvator's Quadrangle.

Two students trudge through a rare snowfall in St Salvator's Quadrangle.

The hearts of the congregation of St Salvator's Chapel are uplifted on a Sunday morning during semesters by the harmonies from the College Choir in the organ loft above. The Choir, which also provides members for the St Leonard's Chapel Choir, is conducted by Dr Bill Stevenson (centre), the University's dedicated organist who has inspired so many students to seek pleasure and relaxation through music.

A gate opens on to St Salvator's College. The North Wing and Lower College Hall were built in the Jacobean style in 1845-46.

It took patience and faith in the east coast weather to get this picture of St Salvator's Quadrangle, with the moon behind, because it reaches this point only one day in the year.

The north wing of St Salvator's College, looking over the Scores, to the bracing North Sea.

The Cathedral in winter, desolate legacy of the Reformation.

St Mary's College, winter, when even the white doves remain inside. Or perhaps they are too well camouflaged.

Fondly known as 'Sally's' to generations of its student occupants, St Salvator's Hall was built through the generosity of the Scottish-American Dr Edward Harkness. The hall was the envy of other European universities when it was opened in 1930.

The medieval Swilken Bridge also leads to the Old Course Hotel.